LIT'

ACTIVISM

THE LITTLE BOOK OF ACTIVISM

An Hachette UK Company
www.hachette.co.uk

Summersdale Publishers Ltd
Part of Octopus Publishing Group Limited
Carmelite House
50 Victoria Embankment
LONDON
EC4Y 0DZ
UK

www.summersdale.com

Printed and bound in Poland

ISBN: 978-1-78783-666-2

The
LITTLE BOOK OF
ACTIVISM

Karen Edwards

Contents

Introduction

Every day, all around us, people are standing up to demand a better world. Whether the means are subtle – through art and petitioning, or more obvious – through protests and demonstrations – at any one time there are thousands, if not millions, of ordinary citizens doing their best to instigate positive change.

The term "activism" originated in the early twentieth century to describe an act that promotes social or political reform. It isn't a recent concept – in fact, societies have been demanding fundamental rights since civilization began. However, recent history has shown us just how vital activism can be in a representative and progressive society.

Activism is everywhere. It's in campaigning for workers' rights, fighting for gender equality, challenging systemic bias and demonstrating against dictatorships. It is in confronting bigotry, ending persecution and protesting against environmental destruction. Activism has also been at the heart of major societal advances – including the dismantling of slavery. There is no doubt it is deeply intertwined in the social progress of the human race.

Most activists are everyday people like you and me, who have compassion for themselves and others. They are able to empathize, and they possess an integrity that leads them to call out injustice when they see it. Most of us, of course, are deeply affected when an issue directly touches us or someone we love. For an activist, this is often what ignites their urge for change.

Any one of us could become a micro-activist by making changes within our own lives. Combine this with support from like-minded people, and that is how macro-activism begins; one person's drive and determination for social justice has often paved the way for powerful movements.

This book will explore the value of activism in all its forms, sharing examples of inspirational social change. We will learn about some of the most influential campaigners, who have inspired millions, and consider how you, too, can become an effective activist, joining the legions of tremendous humans who contribute to making a better world for us all.

TYPES OF ACTIVISM

For centuries, activism has been influential in bringing about reform. In the days of the Roman Empire, slaves would congregate to demand their freedom. Back then, violence and disruption were a common tactic in demanding change, and most rebellions and uprisings would end in bloody battles.

However, over time, the effectiveness of peaceful protest has been recognized, and activism has evolved to include gentler methods of raising awareness. Nowadays, activism can be practised through art, film, dance and crafting – sometimes even in the lyrics of a thought-provoking song. While more traditional methods – such as boycotting, petitioning and picketing – remain popular, wide-ranging alternatives invite anyone to be a part of the peaceful call for change.

As technology has advanced, opportunities for activism have only increased. Social media is used to amplify causes and we can offer immediate support by clicking the "donate" button or sharing a story. Today, activists no longer need to be physically vocal or present at a rally to build awareness.

In this chapter, we will look at various types of peaceful activism that happen every day, uncovering where each originated from and some of the success stories that have resulted from the passionate, creative and diverse work of activists over the years. We will see that while not all activism leads directly to reform, it still holds tremendous value in educating the public, informing them of the plight of those who may not be so fortunate, and highlighting why positive change is needed.

HOW WONDERFUL IT IS THAT NOBODY NEED WAIT A SINGLE MOMENT BEFORE STARTING TO IMPROVE THE WORLD.

ANNE FRANK,
GERMAN DIARIST

Tried-and-tested forms of activism

ARTIVISM	The many different creative techniques of combining art with activism.
CRAFTIVISM	Activism that incorporates the practice of craft, particularly through needlework.
PAMPHLETEERING AND LEAFLETING	The distribution of unbound booklets discussing a cause; used for wide circulation.
PETITIONING	A list of signatures supporting a call for social change or reform.

MICRO-DONATION	A small charitable donation toward a cause; also known as microphilanthropy.
CLICKTIVISM OR DIGITAL ACTIVISM	The use of the internet, especially social media, to gain support for a cause.
ECONOMIC ACTIVISM	The use of economic power to persuade social change and reform.
COLLECTIVE ACTIVISM, PEACEFUL PROTESTS AND DEMONSTRATIONS	A collective action to show support for a cause or to achieve a common objective.

Artivism

For hundreds of years, artists have been using their talent to identify and draw awareness to important social issues. In doing this, they bravely cross the controversial threshold from their role of creators to one of social or political commentators.

Artivism encourages thoughtful conversation around an issue. Engaging with it can be both pleasing and uncomfortable, as it commonly stirs up feelings of vulnerability and a sense of pathos – but these feelings are often instrumental in inspiring public support.

Artivists can appeal directly to followers – whether through social media platforms or in performance spaces – sharing their stance, rallying emotions and discussing personal experiences around an issue. The most powerful work will often be shared on social media over and over again, reaching large international audiences in a matter of hours. By including a simple plea for support alongside their work, an artivist can achieve huge awareness for a cause in a short space of time.

IF WE WANT THE WORLD
TO BE MORE BEAUTIFUL,
KIND AND JUST, THEN
OUR ACTIVISM SHOULD BE
BEAUTIFUL, KIND AND JUST.

SARAH CORBETT,
BRITISH CRAFTIVIST

THE POWER OF MURALS

For over 40,000 years, human beings have been painting murals on cave walls and rocks to document their existence and experience. The beauty of this kind of artwork is that it remains a timeless message that can be studied, analyzed and understood by anyone. Language barriers, cultural misconception and detachment can be somewhat dissolved, allowing any audience to identify with the images they see.

In a rather natural evolution, murals today tend to take the form of street art or graffiti. They still often depict the human experience, and it's not unusual to see scenes of struggle, despair and concern portrayed to raise awareness toward social issues or campaigns. For artivists, the hope is that, by visualizing the problem, the public will be roused into action: share the image, discuss it and perhaps even contribute directly to the campaign.

ARTIVISTS IN ACTION

- British artist Banksy has been anonymously stencilling provocative scenes of human experience through street art in public places for over three decades. His confronting images, which depict topics including slave labour, racism and the plight of refugees, have increased awareness around the world.

- Contemporary artist-turned-artivist Ai Weiwei conveys social issues through sculptures, woodwork and photography. One of his most prominent pieces is a 70-metre-long (230-foot long) inflatable boat carrying 258 faceless refugee figures.

- The *Sea Walls* campaign by international collective Artists for Oceans creates contemporary murals to express the environmental destruction of our oceans due to plastic pollution and climate change. To date, over 400 paintings can be found on walls and the sides of buildings in 17 countries. Their message: "Harness your creativity and help save our oceans."

ON THE BIG AND SMALL SCREEN

The medium of film – showcased through movies, documentaries and television series – is an incredibly powerful form of artivism. It allows the creator to take the viewer on an immersive, investigative journey to uncover information about an issue and learn why social reform could be so important.

Since its invention, film has had many uses, ranging from propaganda to information and entertainment. It has also developed into a trusted method of storytelling: directors, narrators, presenters and actors often work alongside people with lived experience and expert commentators to portray social issues accurately.

By bringing a social issue to life, film-makers are often able to elicit powerful emotions of sadness, frustration, anger and hope from their viewers. The aim to educate and raise awareness is often achieved in a raw but truthful way – usually in the hope that it will lead to direct and passionate support for the cause.

GREAT FILMS ABOUT SOCIAL CHANGE

- Robert Mulligan's 1962 adaptation of *To Kill a Mockingbird* was one of the earliest fictional films to portray prejudice to worldwide audiences. The story of an African-American man sentenced and killed for a crime he did not commit elevated public consciousness of systemic racism.

- Steve McQueen's *12 Years a Slave* (2013) tells the story of Solomon Northup, a New Yorker kidnapped in Washington DC and sold into Louisiana enslavement in 1841. The film is an adaptation of Northup's painful memoir of the same name.

- A light-hearted representation about fighting for social change in Britain, *Made in Dagenham* (2010) tells the story of the 1968 female workers' strikes against gender inequality at the Ford car factory in Essex.

THE TV SHOWS THAT INSPIRE CHANGE

- The 1964 television series *Up,* directed by Michael Apted follows the lives of 14 British children and their families to study how social inequality can determine a young person's future.

- Sir David Attenborough has been successfully raising awareness of the effects of pollution, wildlife poaching and climate change since the 1950s. His work includes *Blue Planet II* (2017) and *A Life on Our Planet* (2020).

- Heartbreaking Netflix miniseries *When They See Us* (2019), directed by Ava duVernay, examines the lives of five young Black and Hispanic men who were falsely prosecuted for rape in 1989. The cast worked closely with the accused – now adults – to demonstrate how wrongful imprisonment affects lives, families and mental health.

- Netflix's *The Edge of Democracy* (2019), by filmmaker Petra Costa, investigates how the controversial politics of presidents Lula, Dilma Rousseff and Jair Bolsonaro have fundamentally altered Brazil's societal well-being.

POWERFUL DOCUMENTARIES THAT INFORM AND ENLIGHTEN

🏴 Michael Moore's 2002 film *Bowling for Columbine* brought international attention to the events surrounding the Columbine High School Massacre in 1999. It addresses the potential causes of the tragedy and examines gun crime in the US.

🏴 The 2017 film *Cries from Syria,* directed by Evgeny Afineesky, is a stark account of the Syrian civil war that has caused the deaths of hundreds of thousands and displaced millions of people. Ordinary citizens, including children, are among the commentators that share their brutal experiences of the Assad regime.

🏴 Gabriela Cowperthwaite's *Blackfish* (2013) conveys the catastrophic consequences of keeping animals captive for human entertainment, by following the life of Tilikum, an orca held at SeaWorld.

ARTIVISM THROUGH THEATRE AND DANCE

For centuries, societies across the world have used performing arts as a form of cultural expression, and in the mid-twentieth century, activism truly gained momentum within theatre and dance, thanks to the progressive Black Arts Movement of the 1960s.

On the stage, a narrative is uniquely adaptable, as traditional plays and well-known stories can be told in a non-traditional way. Dance often leaves issues open to interpretation, allowing viewers to explore their own opinion on matters, while theatre can humanize experiences through visually compelling, in-person storytelling.

A perfect example of this is Shakespeare's *Romeo and Juliet*: the sad tale of a young couple in love, who face dreadful consequences because of their two feuding families. The tragedy that befalls the Montagues and Capulets could easily happen in today's society, perhaps with some modern-day adjustments. What if the two leads were Muslim and Roman Catholic? Or both of the same sex? Showcasing older stories in recognizable settings is a humble reminder to the audience that the issues remain current.

INFLUENTIAL PERFORMANCE ARTIVISM

- Playwright and poet Amiri Baraka, founder of the American Black Arts movement, paved the way for artists to depict oppression and prejudice on stage by opening America's first African-American theatre school in 1965.

- The Broadway production of *OSLO*, detailing the 1993 Oslo Peace Accords between Israelis and Palestinians, brought an important human rights event to mainstream audiences.

- In 2015, the Belarus Free Theatre gave us a glimpse into authoritarian rule by performing unannounced at venues around the UK, encouraging audiences to reflect on how, in some countries, artists are forced to operate underground.

- *Queens of Syria* (2014) combined ancient texts from *The Trojan Women* with accounts from female Syrian refugees to draw the UK audience's awareness toward the unfolding refugee emergency.

THE VALUE OF LITERATURE

Since the eighteenth century, print media has been a crucial tool in activism, used to educate the public on specific issues and share updates on campaign strategies. Pamphlets and flyers (see page 34) condense information into a concise, digestible form. In contrast, newspaper and magazine articles tend to focus on key news angles or first-hand experiences to humanize an issue. They expose the urgency of the problem and often put pressure on decision makers to offer reform.

Both pamphleteering and newspaper articles can be published quickly, and allow the actions of those in power to be scrutinized. Although they take longer to reach publication, books can delve more deeply into each problem and, whether through a lens of fiction or non-fiction, they can study historical events and analyze the reform that is needed to move forward.

Today, the ability to read text online makes literature an accessible and, therefore, even more powerful tool for self-education on an issue. As a result, activist literature can be used to promote a message in all corners of activism.

WRITERS WHO MADE A DIFFERENCE

- Author and abolitionist Harriet Beecher Stowe's (see page 88) global bestseller *Uncle Tom's Cabin* (1852) is a powerful and humanizing story of enslavement that was influential in shifting the perspectives of millions of people in the US and UK.

- George Orwell's *Animal Farm* (1945) laid bare the horrors of Stalin's regime, shedding light on the destruction of communities through political power. Orwell later said that the book attempted to "fuse political purpose and artistic purpose into one whole".

- Journalist and author Amelia Gentleman's 2018 investigation into the Windrush scandal led the UK government to promise compensation and policy reform for the Commonwealth migrants who were invited to live in post-war Britain to rebuild the country's infrastructure, only to be threatened with deportation nearly 50 years later.

THE AUTHORITY OF THE SPOKEN WORD

Every good artist knows that audiences will vary – which means that not all methods of artivism will appeal to everyone. So, while an authoritative piece of writing can be a campaign game-changer with some people, others will prefer to engage with spoken words, such as an impacting address or performed poetry.

Words are a powerful tool. Rallying speeches and impassioned statements have the ability to provoke the public into action, and their descriptive nature can effectively portray social injustice. Speeches can educate and invoke sympathy, as well as establishing an understanding of a complex subject. They can also stir those listening into desiring change. By vocalizing struggle and suffering in a raw, engaging way, speakers can construct a powerful image for those listening. They also provide a voice for people who share similar experiences but may not have the platform, or the strength, to speak out for themselves. Today, passionate discourse remains as vital as ever.

SPEECHES TO REMEMBER

- Delivered from the steps of the Lincoln Memorial in Washington DC, in August 1963, Martin Luther King Jr's "I Have a Dream" speech covered key moments of reform in United States history, before calling for an end to racism toward African Americans.

- Young activist Malala Yousafzai stunned her audience at the UN Youth Takeover 2013 with a moving address demanding quality education for every child.

- After surviving the 2018 Florida high school shooting, 19-year-old Emma Gonzalez addressed a gun control rally, saying: "We are going to be the kids you read about in textbooks. We are going to change the law."

- At the age of 16, Greta Thunberg presented her talk entitled "How Dare You" to the 2019 United Nations Climate Action Summit, in which she questioned why political leaders have yet to declare the enormity of the climate emergency.

ARTIVISM IN SONG

Music is found in every civilization and culture around the world and, much like in art and writing, the human experience has been well-chronicled in song, translating joy and exhilaration, alongside despair and pain. Vocalized music dates back at least as early as the Middle Ages, when Gregorian chanting was first logged. Chants then developed into songs, eventually leading to the delightful lyrical artistry we hear today.

In recent decades, popular musicians – from Bob Marley to Bob Dylan – have dissected social and political injustices through their lyrics, delivering inspired and passionate demonstrations for the causes close to their hearts.

While many music fans encourage an artist's desire to express their feelings and beliefs through song, others argue that musicians should entertain only, and not cross the line into political or social realms. However, despite the occasional controversy, music – particularly in more recent decades – has been fundamental in raising awareness and rallying for reform.

MESSAGES THROUGH MUSIC

- Blues artist Johnny Cash was one of the original greats to take on the artivist role in the 1960s by performing televised shows and recording a live album (*At Folsom Prison*) in US jails to raise awareness for the human rights abuses faced by prisoners.

- Nina Simone's "To Be Young, Gifted and Black" (1970) is a gentle song with an empowering message to African Americans and the global Black community: that being Black is a gift and carries immense worth.

- Californian rockers Rage Against The Machine – whose name is a political message in itself – attracted universal media coverage when they performed their track "Sleep Now in the Fire", about greed and social injustice, outside the New York Stock Exchange in 2000.

- John Lennon's "Imagine" (1971) asked listeners to envision a world with no war, greed, poverty, materialism and division due to religion. The song became one of the most performed tracks of the twentieth century.

- Millions of people watched in awe as British grime artist Dave used his platform at the 2020 BRIT Awards to perform his track "Black", which storifies the systemic racism faced by Black people.

MUSIC EXPRESSES THAT WHICH CANNOT BE SAID AND ON WHICH IT IS IMPOSSIBLE TO BE SILENT.

VICTOR HUGO,
FRENCH POET, NOVELIST
AND DRAMATIST

The subtle power of craftivism

Craftivism allows messages around social reform to be explored through the creative pursuits of needlework, sculpting, jewellery-making, pottery and even yarn bombing – and it can encourage more thoughtful decision-making from those in power. It is truly a dynamic, gentle and respectful way to open a conversation around an issue.

The term "craftivism" was coined in 2003 by Betsy Greer, an American writer who is a major advocate for the goodness within crafting. At the time, she wrote, "Each time you participate in crafting you are making a difference, whether it's fighting against useless materialism or making items for charity or something betwixt and between."

In contrast to the loud and demonstrative action of a protest, craftivism encourages quiet engagement with issues and is becoming a popular, non-intrusive method of activist communication. The calmness of crafting can also act as a form of healing for activists themselves, who can channel emotions such as fear and anger into patience and reflection.

CRAFT IN ACTION

- Judy Chicago's 1974–1979 installation, *The Dinner Party*, featured 39 embroidered place settings on a table runner, showcasing the names of remarkable women in history, alongside their valued accomplishments.

- In New South Wales, Australia, Knitting Nannas Against Gas peacefully protest against environmental destruction for non-renewable energy use. They sell their hand-knitted beanies, scarves and badges, and gather at planning permission hearings to share their craftwork.

- In 2018, craftivist Salma Zulfiqar from Birmingham, UK, began working with local refugees to make a stitched quilt entitled *The Migration Blanket*. The finished product is a startlingly honest patchwork showcase of what a lack of safety feels like, alongside hopes for the future.

Pamphleteering and leafleting

Thought to be among the first printed materials in Western Europe, pamphlets – defined as unbound publications (not periodicals) that contained no fewer than five and no more than 48 pages – were developed during the early sixteenth century to share controversial religious and political propaganda.

While traditional pamphlets aren't used as often by modern-day activists, leaflets and flyers are still commonly distributed by charities and organizations to educate readers – often in connection to a website – and rally more engagement. It is commonly argued that blogging is a new-age version of pamphleteering, because of the personal perspective that each post can give.

Without regulation, pamphleteering (and blogging) can enable the spread of misinformation or give rise to unpleasant rhetoric. Used well, however, it is a great tool for research and education, and can inspire new ideas for social change in a community setting. Thanks to substantiated information online, both mediums can now also be easily verified. Best of all, it enables campaigners to reach all corners of society, encouraging grassroots – or citizen – activism to grow.

POWERFUL PAMPHLETEERS

- Theologian John Calvin rallied for the sixteenth-century Protestant Reformation by distributing controversial pamphlets which exposed errors and abuses by the Catholic Church.

- In the early seventeenth century, English writer Thomas Dekker shared fictional depictions and factual accounts about life in London (*Plague Pamphlets*), wryly subjecting readers to his political partiality.

- In the eighteenth century, abolitionist William Fox printed 250,000 pamphlets to encourage the boycott of sugar produced using slave labour. "In every pound of sugar used we may be considered as consuming two ounces of human flesh," he wrote.

Petitioning

Petitions have contributed to progressive dialogues and social change for centuries. In fact, according to a 2019 study by the UK's Arts and Humanities Research Council, in England petitioning was "ubiquitous" as far back as the seventeenth century, with thousands of civilians viewing a petition as an important way to communicate with authorities.

Over 400 years later, petitions are still one of the most common ways to call for reform, and e-petitions make signing and submission even easier. In the UK, British citizens or residents can publish a petition calling for specific reforms on the Government and Parliament website – the issue will be considered for a parliamentary debate if it reaches 100,000 signatures. Meanwhile, in the United States, the First Amendment of the American Constitution gives Americans the right to petition to the federal government.

Does petitioning work? Sometimes it does, sometimes it doesn't – but regardless of the direct outcome, it still sends a powerful message to the relevant authorities, showing that there is a notable public demand for change.

PETITION WINS

- More than a million people signed an Amnesty International petition to free pregnant Meriam Ibrahim, who was sentenced to death in Sudan for marrying a Christian man. She was freed in 2014.

- Caroline Criado-Perez led the 2014 petition to feature women on UK banknotes, which resulted in the new £10 note featuring novelist Jane Austen and the new Scottish £5 note picturing author Nan Shepard.

- A call to increase support for refugees in the UK was signed by 450,287 people. In 2015, Prime Minister David Cameron confirmed that the UK would welcome 20,000 more Syrian refugees under the Vulnerable Person Relocation scheme and spend a further £100 million on humanitarian aid.

- During the Covid-19 outbreak in 2020, a petition seeking urgent resources for Indigenous Canadian communities gathered nearly 60,000 signatures, leading the government to assign them an additional $305 million for healthcare.

Micro-donation: the act of giving

The instinct to help those less fortunate is a wonderful part of human nature. Early philanthropy was typically instigated by religious organizations, and covered basics such as food, shelter and essential hygiene supplies. By the mid-twentieth century, funding was needed to support the growing number of global humanitarian programmes – so televised infomercials, billboard posters and public collections were launched by recognized charities in the UK and US. Each one had a common message: "Please give what you can."

This led to the development of the micro-donation platforms we know today, such as text-to-give, click-to-donate, the Pennies system (see opposite), GoFundMe and Facebook fundraisers. The minimal payment means that individuals from all social groups can become activists. Once engaged, donors are invited to follow the campaign journey by opting in to receive updates from the organizers.

Micro-donation has proved vital in humanitarian crises, when relief organizations often depend on significant funding at short notice to provide emergency aid distributions. Members of the public can use grassroots crowdfunding platforms, such as GoFundMe or JustGiving, to raise money for personal causes.

ONE MICRO-DONATION AT A TIME

- The Pennies foundation allows customers to use card machines to donate between one penny and 99 pence to UK charities. To date, Pennies has raised over £25 million in donations for more than 600 British charities.

- HOPE is an animal shelter that has raised nearly $150,000 through GoFundMe. The organization not only protects Rio de Janeiro's street dogs, but it also empowers the homeless community who staff the shelter, giving them skills to help them transition to permanent employment.

- UK veterinary company Medivet raised over £500,000 toward their Saving The Rhino campaign, which supports the protection of African rhinos from poachers. Clients were offered the option of making a small charitable donation – 50 pence – when visiting a Medivet veterinary practice.

- A public GoFundMe campaign set up in the wake of the 2018 Tree of Life Synagogue shooting in Pittsburgh, Pennsylvania, raised over $1 million to assist survivors, victims' families and the repair of physical damage to the building.

- Shopping app Give As You Live raises money by charging retailers commission for clicks. When customers spend money via the app, they can choose which charity the commission goes to.

ALONE WE CAN DO SO
LITTLE, TOGETHER WE
CAN DO SO MUCH.

HELEN KELLER,
AMERICAN AUTHOR,
DISABILITY RIGHTS ADVOCATE
AND POLITICAL ACTIVIST

Clicktivism

Working hand-in-hand with micro-donation and e-petitioning, clicktivism – or digital activism – refers to the use of the internet to raise awareness of social issues. Clicktivism began in the late 1990s, when the simple action of sending an email could spread activist agendas. Now, with channels such as Facebook, Twitter and Instagram – each boasting millions of users – activists have gained much wider-reaching platforms.

However, there is a downside to clicktivism: it requires little commitment from the user to support reform. This kind of "slacktivism", in the form of an easy "like" or share, can lead to the distribution of misinformation, such as in the 2020 #blackouttuesday campaign. While some users understood that the posting of black squares on Instagram, triggered by anti-racism protests in the US, was a specific act of solidarity instigated by the music industry, others did not. As a result, social media was flooded with black squares under the hashtag #blacklivesmatter, which many people assumed was associated, even though it was a separate campaign. This diluted the Black Lives Matter movement's messaging to their demonstrators.

HASHTAGGING FOR REFORM

- The 2017 hashtag #MeToo showed just how powerful clicktivism can be when channelled well. As millions of people – both famous and from the general public – shared their experiences of sexual assault, the universal scale of the issue was f inally recognized.

- Artivists across the world use #paintforapurpose on Instagram to promote their powerful depictions of issues. With a short caption underneath, posts have the potential to reach thousands upon thousands of Instagram users.

- During the 2020 anti-racism demonstrations, Black Lives Matter – which advocates peaceful protests against incidents of police brutality and systemic racism – shared news of daily rally locations and times via their #blacklivesmatter hashtag.

Economic activism

Using consumer clout to push for reform is a common measure taken by grassroots activists. It involves boycotting companies that do not support a particular issue while choosing organizations that do. Businesses, too, can drive positive social change by pledging their alliance to and supporting a cause. Often, such engagement is picked up by the media, drawing positive attention to both the issue and the company.

Economic activism dates back to the late eighteenth century, when an international boycott of products made by slave labour – known as the Free Produce Movement – began. Initially launched in British Quaker circles, the message spread quickly, with activist William Fox using pamphleteering to call the boycott. This peaceful yet powerful remonstration was an important chapter in the eventual abolition of slavery.

Examples of current-day economic activism include the boycott of beauty products tested on animals and the avoidance of establishments that permit cruelty to wildlife, e.g. by training wild animals to entertain audiences. Veganism – now a widely practiced lifestyle choice that involves not purchasing or consuming animal products – helps to prevent livestock cruelty and decreases the impact of farming on the environment.

THE BEST BOYCOTTS AND BUSINESS PLANS

- George – a UK supermarket fashion retailer – announced a 2020 partnership with the charity Diversity Role Models to coincide with the supermarket's "Being You" initiative. Its aim was to guarantee diversity and inclusivity in its advertising and workplace.

- The International Marine Mammal Project's 1986 campaign, which boycotted the purchase of yellowfin tuna because of unethical fishing practices, eventually led fisheries to stop using the "dolphin scooping" method.

- UK supermarket Aldi impressed customers in 2016 by pledging to remove unsustainable palm oil from all own-brand products and making its supply chain public.

- From the 1960s, Britons were a part of the international Boycott Movement that lasted for over thirty years. The aim was to take a stand against apartheid in South Africa by not purchasing its produce, such as fruit, cigarettes and sherry. Supermarkets Tesco and Sainsbury's even stopped stocking the goods.

- Several US companies – including United Airlines, Hertz and Best Western – were forced to cut ties with the National Rifle Association (NRA), due to widespread consumer boycotts. This happened after the NRA spoke out against student activists who called for better gun control laws, following the Parkland High School shooting in 2018.

Collective activism

For thousands of years, collective activism – the action taken by one or several groups to call for social, political, economic or environmental reform – has been effective in pursuing change.

Collective activism – such as protests, marches, pickets to strikes, boycotts and vigils – tends to happen when societal injustice reaches a tipping point. People who have been oppressed or experienced inequality for a long time are joined in their pursuit for reform by those who aren't directly affected but feel strongly about the cause. Such mass action allows for the sharing of stories and experiences within a like-minded community, which can be cathartic as well as galvanizing for activists.

In 2003, over 30 million people rallied in nearly 800 cities in 72 countries around the world to protest the planned invasion of Iraq. While the "We Are Many" march could not stop the invasion, it remains one of the largest demonstrations of collective, peaceful activism in history.

CONTROVERSIAL COLLECTIVE

Extinction Rebellion (XR for short) are an international environmental campaign group that have asked governments around the world to declare a climate and ecological emergency. The group was co-founded in 2018 by environmentalists Gail Bradbrook and Roger Hallam, to demand immediate action to address climate change.

Extinction Rebellion have been clear about what needs to be done to combat climate change. As well as making the public aware of the seriousness of the issue, they propose that the UK should aim to reduce carbon emissions to "net zero" by 2025.

The group's organized protests have been somewhat divisive: in 2019, one demonstration brought the City of London to a standstill over 11 days, and in 2020, a rally outside three of London's presses prevented the printing of some weekend newspapers. While their call to action is generally respected – and well-publicized in the UK – their tendency toward civil disobedience hasn't always gone down well with the general public or Parliament.

FIVE PROTESTS THAT CHANGED THE WORLD

1. THE BOSTON TEA PARTY (1773)

At the time, America consisted of 13 British colonies, where citizens were forced to buy imported goods at high prices. On 16 December, the "Sons of Liberty" broke into a British ship, stole 342 crates of tea and dumped it all into the harbour. This act of civil disobedience led to the American Revolution and, in turn, America's independence.

2. THE STORMING OF THE BASTILLE (1789)

These violent remonstrations began after French civilians grew frustrated at the authoritarian rule by their monarchy. The invasion of a state prison in Paris led to a battle that ended in the murder of a high-profile governor. The attack marked the beginning of the French Revolution and the monarchy was replaced by a republic in 1799. This is now celebrated as Bastille Day on 14 July.

3. THE FIRST US RALLY FOR WOMEN'S SUFFRAGE (1913)

Leading American suffragists combined pamphleteering, speech-giving and boycotting campaigns with collective activism to win women the right to vote in federal elections. In 1920, women were granted the vote in the United States.

4. ANTI-VIETNAM WAR DEMONSTRATIONS (1965–1970)

Protests against the Vietnam War began as small campaigns in 1965, when the news of the United States' first bomb-strike on North Vietnam began to spread. As the war expanded, so did the protests, with marches, demonstrations and sit-ins becoming increasingly common.

5. PEOPLE'S CLIMATE MARCH (2014)

On 21 September, an estimated 600,000 people attended 156 global marches against climate change, making it the largest climate protest to date. The march was planned as a peaceful response to an upcoming United Nations Climate Summit, indicating to world leaders that ordinary citizens realized the importance of protecting the planet.

WE HAVE TO BE VISIBLE... WE HAVE TO SHOW THE WORLD THAT WE ARE NUMEROUS.

SYLVIA RIVERA,
TRANSGENDER DRAG QUEEN
AND CIVIL RIGHTS ACTIVIST

HOW TO BE
AN EFFECTIVE
ACTIVIST

One of the greatest strengths you possess as a human being is the ability to change things for the better. By using your privilege and good fortune to improve the lives of others, you can achieve truly valuable and wonderful things.

In this chapter, we will discuss the qualities that make an empowered and effective activist, and consider the ways in which you can support the issues that matter to you, in a way that you find comfortable. We will explore how effective action often starts with everyday micro-activism – for instance, by modifying your lifestyle or the attitudes within your own household.

While it may not always seem like your voice is being heard or that progress is being made, recognize that not all change is obvious. Never underestimate the quiet contemplation of the unheard public known as "the silent majority" – the people who are engaged with current issues, but don't voice their opinions as activists. Most importantly, believe that reform is possible – and that you can be one of the wonderful souls who helps to create a happy, flourishing society.

YOU MUST NEVER BE
FEARFUL ABOUT WHAT
YOU ARE DOING WHEN
IT IS RIGHT.

ROSA PARKS,
CIVIL RIGHTS CAMPAIGNER

Educate yourself

The key to becoming an effective activist is to truly understand the topic you are campaigning about. After all, if you hope to educate others on the subject, it is best to have a wealth of factual information, statistics and examples to back up your reasoning.

Read widely – from books to verified news sources – listen to podcasts and watch documentaries and films on the topic you are supporting (you'll find some valuable resources on page 140). If in doubt: research, research, research. Talk to people who have experienced the issue in question – even if you already have a personal understanding. Listening to different perspectives will help to build a well-rounded idea of the subject from various viewpoints and highlight the areas that need prioritizing for action.

If you speak with confidence, people will listen and value the factual information you are sharing. However, you don't have to know *everything* about the issue straightaway, especially as causes evolve with time. Be open about your desire to learn, understand and listen – and practise all of these things.

Identify your perspective

Many of us are driven toward activism because of a personal connection to a social issue. Perhaps we have experienced a form of prejudice or we have seen the devastating human suffering resulting from the rising sea level and climate change.

But what if we don't have a direct connection to a cause? Should we feel we have no business in showing support? Is it "not our problem"? Ideally, we should feel secure in standing up for an issue we care about because *everyone* is responsible for creating a better world. Everyone will reap the benefits if we strive for social good and to create the foundations of a secure and contented society.

The best way to establish your stance on a topic is to come up with a personal mission statement. It doesn't have to be more than a sentence or two, but it should encapsulate why you care about the issue. Doing this will also help you to communicate your feelings to others.

It can be nerve-wracking to introduce a conversation on a serious social issue to friends and family – especially if you know they may disagree with your point of view. However, you should have confidence in your opinions. Remember: the reason many people are detached from a cause is often simply because they haven't thought about it from a personal perspective, aren't aware of it or don't understand it, so most are likely to welcome an enlightening discussion.

An example is the continuing anti-racism movement and the question of whether those who haven't experienced racial prejudice should offer observations or speak up on the issue. The truth is that the more allies willing to stand against every type of prejudice, the better, so don't be afraid to show support. After all, we have one collective goal – to make the world a friendlier place for everyone. To make that happen, we need more advocates for kindness, inclusion and positive change.

Regardless of your experiences, be proud to stand for a cause that is compassionate, progressive and, ultimately, *good*.

Conscious activism

Activism by doing – also known as conscious activism – is a wonderful way of leading by example. If you are hoping to introduce positive social reform into everyday life, there is nothing more powerful than showing people *how* to make changes successfully.

It allows others to see potential changes in a real-world setting that could easily be a part of their routine or household. Conscious activism is particularly useful when advocating for lifestyle-based change – such as eating more sustainably, abolishing single-use plastics or speaking up against prejudice.

Consider documenting the adaptations you make on a personal blog or social media to showcase the effectiveness of your work. Explain your decisions to those around you and share your sources of information, such as books, articles or YouTube videos, so that others can benefit from them, too. This will inspire people to adopt similar measures, and they will realize that supporting a cause is achievable and worthwhile.

Join forces with like-minded souls

Being an activist might seem like a one-person fight at times, but it certainly doesn't have to be that way. If you're feeling in need of connection, you may find it useful to team up with like-minded individuals who are looking for a similar sense of camaraderie.

You could do this by asking organizations or activists in your community for connections, or by approaching social media groups that support the same issues.

By uniting with others who feel as passionately about a cause as you do, you can contribute your skills, build a valuable support network and bounce ideas off each other. Plus, there is the possibility of making new friends who truly understand your interests and with whom you can share this unique campaigning experience. This will share the load and also make life as an activist so much more enjoyable – knowing that others are championing the same cause will offer you hope for a more just future.

Maintain balance

While raising awareness and highlighting the need for reform is important, it can also be exhausting and, sometimes, emotionally draining work. In reality, when we become heavily invested in a cause, it might be hard to separate such heartfelt effort from everyday life.

Before you pledge yourself to an activist's lifestyle, make a clear plan of how many hours per week you intend to dedicate to the cause, ensuring that you balance this evenly with work and social activities. Use a weekly diary to highlight the days and times you wish to give to activism. If you plan to attend an event, take that time out of your activism diary on another day.

Time management is crucial when juggling multiple commitments, so ensure you specifically allocate time for exercise, hobbies and loved ones, and stick to it. Understand that, while being an activist is a wonderful thing, it is imperative to take breaks, clear your mind and prioritize self-care. You will be a more effective activist if you are healthy, well-rested and relaxed.

FOUR STEPS TO BEING A MINDFUL ACTIVIST

🚩 Schedule fun activities, such as a day out with friends or family, to avoid becoming too consumed by your activist commitments. Do your activism "work" only on the days you have assigned to it.

🚩 Some issues can be hard to hear about constantly, and you may find yourself emotionally affected. If so, ensure you take regular breaks; step outside, breathe in the fresh air and clear your mind.

🚩 Meditation, yoga and spending time around nature can help to clear your mind when you're feeling overwhelmed. Exercise can also help to improve your emotional well-being.

🚩 Counteract moments of futility with expressions of gratitude by writing down three things you are grateful for at the end of each day.

Manage expectations

Activist movements have contributed to many of the positive social reforms in history, but it is important to remember that most of those changes took years, if not decades or centuries, to come about. This is more the case for national reform, such as the US women's rights movement, which began in the nineteenth centruy with pioneering suffragist Elizabeth Cady Stanton leading the way. It wasn't until 1920 that the Nineteenth Amendment to the US Constitution was made (giving women in the US the right to vote) and, in many ways, we are still fighting this cause today.

When embarking on activism, bear in mind that there may not be immediate results. Prepare yourself for a long road ahead and celebrate the little wins – such as community recognition, a great turnout to events, the rise of grassroots advocacy, meeting fundraising targets, receiving media coverage and growing support from the public. Find joy in the fact that you are educating people and making a difference on an individual basis – that counts for a lot.

Withstand opposition

Unfortunately, activists sometimes find themselves on the receiving end of unfavourable behaviour from those who disagree with their views. This can be disheartening and, occasionally, painful to experience – but in these times, it's important to stay focused on why you are supporting the cause.

Understand that those expressing such negativity are usually only doing so because they are unable to put their point across in a calm and pleasant manner. According to Professor Julinna Oxley, writer of the essay "How to Be a (Good) Philosopher-Activist", in order to be a good activist, it is vital to be able to "listen to another person and respond to them without overreacting, being defensive, belittling them or losing one's cool", as well as "knowing when to make an objection and knowing when to let something go".

Remember: not everyone can be persuaded to support an issue – but a composed response when challenged with hostility will be respected by those listening to both sides of the argument and may plant a seed that can flourish later on.

Activism for introverts

Not all of us were born to be confident speech-givers or rally organizers, so how does someone with a quieter personality become an effective activist? The truth is, you don't have to be loud to be influential – and you certainly don't need to lead movements to make a difference. In fact, many of the people you are trying to reach are likely to be introverts, too (around a half of us are).

In her inspiring 2016 TED Talk entitled "Activism Needs Introverts", British craftivist Sarah Corbett highlights how the shy ones among us can be brilliant at more intimate activism and are valuable in carrying out behind-the-scenes work.

Taking part in craft and artivism projects, pamphleteering, petitioning, micro-donations, clicktivism and (quiet) boycotting are all great ways to commit to a cause without having to put yourself in a confrontational situation. Social media posts are a resourceful way to show your support without having to shout too loudly. You might be pleasantly surprised by how successful gentle activism can be at reaching wide audiences.

IDEAS FOR THE QUIET ACTIVISTS

1. Try your hand at knitting or painting – you can sell your art or craftivism to raise money for your cause, or use it to share a message.

2. Start a blog about your activism journey and share your emotions, experiences and schedule with your network.

3. Start a podcast at home – all you really need is a microphone and, if you're feeling fancy, a pop shield. Pick an angle for each episode, and maybe even invite fellow activists to join you.

4. Verify information with charities and organizations, before creating a simple website with your findings and sources. You might end up being a valuable resource to many people.

5. We discussed this in more detail on the conscious activism page (page 58), but living by example truly is the best way to advocate for your cause.

Behind-the-scenes support

A common misconception is that you have to be on the front line of activism to make a difference. While loud, bold activism does get a lot of attention, it is important to remember that behind every outspoken face, there is often a team of people helping to bring their message to the public.

There is a place for all of us in creating positive change. If you are more of a behind-the-scenes person by nature, don't be afraid to focus on this, because every role is vital in raising awareness and pushing for reform. Don't hesitate to bring your natural skills to the table – whether they are administrative, organizational or creative – and lend a hand where necessary.

Rest assured that whatever you are able to contribute will be valued – every little bit helps when setting the activism cogs in motion. While the quieter, more subtle, tasks may not put you in the limelight, they are essential for the effective functioning of any campaign.

ROLES OF UNSUNG HEROES

- Event planning or organizing fundraisers.

- Designing flyers, literature or web pages to share information.

- Letter, speech and blog writing for those who are the face of the campaign.

- Putting together presentations for the frontline activists to use in the public domain.

- Volunteering to drive campaign leaders to and from appointments.

- Looking after the accounting and budgeting.

- Using your knowledge or skill in art or craft to introduce artivism or craftivism initiatives to your fellow activists.

- Managing social media platforms to share the work that your team are doing.

- Signing and sharing the campaign's e-petitions.

- Sharing verified information on an issue via social media channels.

Write letters and articles

If you feel passionately about a cause, consider putting your thoughts down on paper. Not only are articles and letters powerful ways to inspire others to see things from your point of view, but writing can also be incredibly therapeutic when feeling overwhelmed, disappointed or affected by a cause.

Once you feel informed on the issue, consider writing honestly about it in an article for a local newspaper, community newsletter or noticeboard. You could also address it to someone in a position of power, such as a local Member of Parliament, a consumer manager (who is typically responsible for the running of a business or marketing of a product) or board member. Most decision makers are voted into position by a committee or the general public, so it is in their best interest to acknowledge what you, a member of the public, have to say. Plus, there's no force involved, and seeing facts and figures written down will often stick in someone's memory far better than spoken statistics.

TIPS FOR WRITING TO DECISION MAKERS

- Limit your letter to a page so that even the busiest of bosses will have time to read it.

- Be as clear as possible on the issue you are supporting – don't assume that the person you're writing to knows its background or context.

- If you're responding to a recent decision or event, then do so within a few days. This is also relevant if you're addressing a particular issue in a newspaper or newsletter.

- Discuss how the issue affects you or your community, and tell the decision maker why you are appealing to them and how they could make a positive difference. The onus is then on them to consider their next move.

- Even if you are feeling sad or angry about an issue, it's important to remain level-headed when addressing the problem. Leave out heated or dramatic language.

Embrace grassroots activism

Grassroots activism – or citizen-based activism – involves planting that seed of awareness within the public domain and then watering it with information, education and opportunity, with the vision that it will grow into a successful campaign for change.

This might mean attending social gatherings, where you can introduce the issue in question into discussions, or joining a community team that is already centred around advocating for local causes. There may also be a newsletter or group flyer you could contribute to.

Remember: while localized grassroots activists are often dismissed as being inconsequential or "small fry", this couldn't be further from the truth. If an increasing number of community members are calling for reform, those in power are more likely to listen – and change is more likely to occur.

THE VALUE OF A GRASSROOTS CAMPAIGN

🚩 It introduces the topic into a community forum, making the issue more visible and encouraging people to form an opinion – and to voice it. This means it becomes much harder to ignore or brush under the carpet.

🚩 It uses valuable public clout to pursue reform. Decision makers know it is the general public who are voting them into power. It is in their interest to keep their community happy.

🚩 It is best supported by activism from home, such as art and craftivism, e-petitioning, micro-donation and clicktivism. Plus, it is easier than ever to encourage the public to fight for reform from the comfort of their sofas.

🚩 It brings a community together in their battle for a common cause. This is a beautiful thing and can only serve people well, as friendships are made and networks are expanded on a local level.

The value of allyship

To become an ally is to stand in solidarity with those affected by a specific social issue without judgement. This might mean seeking out the voices of those who are disadvantaged to understand their experiences and then sharing those experiences to actively challenge misinformed attitudes.

Allyship means more than making generalized statements against the problem – it means using your privilege (the fact that you don't suffer as a result of the issue) to call out injustice when you see it. Allies are welcome, needed and valued.

When stepping into an ally role, make sure to be sensitive and to listen, while avoiding projecting your personal thoughts onto others. Remember that less advantaged people have been campaigning for their own rights for centuries – it is often built into their heritage and story – and understand that the feeling of continuous injustice over generations can be exhausting. By standing in unity, you are saying, "I've got your back, and I can carry your torch for a while."

FIVE SIMPLE WAYS TO BE A GREAT ALLY

- Allyship should begin as an internal action. Ensure that you, too, are unbiased in your judgement.

- Actively seek out marginalized perspectives, in order to learn more about people's lived experiences.

- This shouldn't be a performative action. Don't jump on an activism bandwagon because everyone else is doing it. Do it because you believe in justice – and care that the situation changes for the better.

- Be strong in your stance. If you see or hear bigotry, call it out confidently by tapping into your educated understanding of the issue.

- Be prepared for the fact that not everyone will understand your viewpoint straightaway, but know that you can use your knowledge to educate them on *why* you feel this way. Be proud that you are standing up for what's right and just.

Use the power of democracy

We already know that activism, ultimately, seeks reform. Consequently, one of the most meaningful actions you can make as an activist is to vote for the government – both local and national – who will implement the change you want.

MAKING AN INFORMED CHOICE

- Empower yourself by researching the policies behind each election candidate.

- Consider candidates' positions on the issues that matter most to you, as well as other vital issues. It is unlikely that a candidate will be perfect, but one may be more aligned with your views.

- If you are eligible, make sure you register to vote.

- If you're unable to vote in person, you may be able to register for a postal vote or to assign a proxy, in advance.

- If you feel particularly strongly in favour of one candidate, consider volunteering to assist their local campaign.

Inspire the next generation

1. SPEAKING OUT IS OK

Discuss the importance of speaking out about wrongdoing, even when it might feel uncomfortable. Perhaps offer younger children a specific example, such as how they might feel if they were told off for the mess someone else made. Wouldn't they want a friend to stand up for them?

2. EXPLORE DISCRIMINATION

Be aware of using stereotypes, or suggesting a link between appearance and behavioural traits, which could cause kids to become unconsciously biased. Normalize everyday distinctions by explaining how sometimes people can look or dress differently to them, have families who look different to theirs, or might not walk or talk like them. Discussions about empathy and how it might feel when someone is left out of a game are useful, too.

3. THE REAL HEROES

There are many wonderful children's books about prominent activists, some of which are listed on page xx. If possible, read books about campaigners your child can identify with – perhaps of the same gender, or with a similar hair or skin colour. Remind them that the story is about a real person who really achieved those things, and that we can do the same if we want to.

4. BECOME A TRAILBLAZER

If your passion for a cause encourages you to become increasingly involved in activism, you might find yourself becoming the unassuming leader of a local movement. While this prospect might seem daunting, it's important to remember that an effective leader often has a team of supporters behind them (page 66) – so you aren't tackling this alone.

Leaders are vital in a campaign because they step forward as the role model and the face of a cause. By communicating truthfully and honestly about their experiences and aims, they are able to inspire the people who are watching and listening.

Team members are also likely to look to you for inspiration, messaging and strategy – so leading with decency and kindness is important. The measures you choose to promote awareness will likely be adopted by your team. Whether you are quietly writing letters to the local Member of Parliament, creating works of art, posting flyers or staging a small protest outside the local council offices, acting in a peaceful and thoughtful manner will always serve you well.

QUALITIES OF A BRILLIANT LEADER

🏴 **Share your passion and your knowledge**
   Tell people why you care about the issue. However personal it is, this is a genuine and humbling way of garnering support.

⚑ Be a role model

You are representing the change you want to see, so practise the same reform – whether through lifestyle, conversation or attitude – at home.

⚑ Communicate clearly

Openly share your hopes, ideas and plans to keep your followers updated. You might do this through social media posts and e-newsletter subscriptions or by speaking directly to supporters at organized events.

⚑ Try new things

There are so many wonderful ways to approach activism. If one method doesn't work so well, don't be put off – simply try something else.

⚑ Encourage individuality and creativity

Everyone has a different way of showing support, so embolden your followers to contribute in the way they feel most comfortable. Tell them that, whether they are demonstrating, donating or dancing, their efforts are invaluable.

I BELIEVE IN CHANGE.
I BELIEVE IN THE POWER
IT HAS TO UNITE US
AND IGNITE US.

UZO ADUBA,
NIGERIAN-AMERICAN ACTRESS

FAMOUS ACTIVISTS AND SOCIAL CHANGES

Throughout the centuries, people of all ages and genders have been stepping up every day to campaign for a better world. That brave and fearless urge to educate others and highlight the need for reform has resulted in some of the world's most impactful social and political movements – many of which have gone on to alter the way in which we live our lives.

From the international campaigns to establish women's suffrage and the civil rights activists standing against prejudice, to the individuals fighting to help disadvantaged communities and to de-escalate the climate crisis – all kinds of people have gone on to become advocates for awareness, kindness, equality, peace and social good.

In this chapter, we will celebrate a selection of peaceful activists who have led us – often after many years of struggle – to an improved way of life. We will discover how their passion was ignited and how they used their platform to rally support, as well as the setbacks they faced and, ultimately, how one person's desire for greater good evolved into something bigger than anyone could have ever imagined.

THE ABOLITIONIST MOVEMENT (c.1783–1865)

It is estimated that 10–12 million people were sold to slave owners in England, Western Europe and America from the sixteenth to the nineteenth century. Abolition was the transatlantic movement to end the slave trade and enslavement.

KEY MOMENTS

1619 – The first African slaves arrive in Virginia.

1774–1804 – US Northern States abolish slavery.

1787 – British anti-slavery sentiment rises, spurred by abolitionist Thomas Clarkson.

1808 – US Congress outlaws the African slave trade, but domestic trading continues.

1831 – A network of people assisting in freeing the enslaved, known as the Underground Railroad, gains impetus in the US.

1833 – The Slavery Abolition Act is introduced in England and takes effect by mid-1834.

1833– A law is passed to abolish slavery across the British Empire, which would go on to free 800,000 people.

1850 – The US Fugitive Slave Act allows runaways to be captured and returned to owners.

1852 – Author Harriet Beecher Stowe publishes *Uncle Tom's Cabin*, humanizing the enslaved for white readers.
1863 – Abraham Lincoln's Emancipation Proclamation changes the status of over four million slaves to "free".

1865 – The Thirteenth Amendment to the US Constitution, abolishing slavery, is passed in January and ratified in December.

Thomas Clarkson

NAME: Thomas Clarkson (1760–1846)
NATIONALITY: British
ACTIVISM: Abolitionist

In 1785, Cambridgeshire-born Thomas Clarkson won a Latin essay-writing competition on whether enslavement was lawful. Studying first-hand accounts of those in the slave trade meant that the horrifying details were forever embedded in his mind.

In 1786 his essay was translated into English and published, attracting the attention of pioneering abolitionists such as Granville Sharp, who was already campaigning to end the slave trade. The pair co-founded the Committee for the Abolition of the African Slave Trade in 1787, and together they persuaded the MP for Hull, William Wilberforce, to join their cause.

In his mission to gather eyewitness accounts, Clarkson travelled across the country to the harbours where slave ships were docked, including the famous ports of Bristol and Liverpool, to interview around 20,000 sailors.

He collected equipment from onboard the ships - such as shackles, handcuffs, thumbscrews and branding irons - with the intention of presenting this evidence to Parliament and the public. In 1787, he published the pamphlet, *A Summary View of the Slave Trade and of the Probable Consequences of Its Abolition*, before continuing to collect even more proof for his case against the slave trade.

Clarkson's findings caused a public shockwave, enabling Wilberforce to motion abolition to Parliament almost every year. The Napoleonic Wars in 1803 meant the temporarily ceasing of their campaign. However, Clarkson and his activist allies returned to work in 1804. Just three years later, the Slave Trade Act of 1807 - outlawing the Atlantic slave trade - was passed in England, with the US bill following shortly after.

In 1823, Clarkson travelled again, this time amassing 777 petitions to Parliament and demanding the liberation of all slaves. The 1833 Slavery Abolition Act emancipated all enslaved people in Britain, and from 1834, slaves were freed from the colonies. Clarkson continued his campaign until his death in 1846.

Harriet Tubman

NAME: Harriet Tubman (c.1820–1913)
NATIONALITY: American
ACTIVISM: Abolitionist

There is no record of Harriet Tubman's birth into slavery at a Maryland plantation. However, her memories have helped to paint the traumatic picture of her early years.

She was just five years old when she was first hired to look after an infant – her first job away from her mother. Tubman would later recall how she was whipped around the neck each time the baby cried. Eventually, weak due to malnourishment, she was sent back to her parents. She then contracted measles after spending long periods each day in waist-deep water, collecting muskrats from traps.

At eight years old, Tubman ran away from her mistress after taking a lump of sugar. In fear of punishment, she hid in a pig pen for days, eating scraps before returning home. Finally, at the age of 12, she was sent to work in the fields – a job she said she preferred to domestic chores handed out by slave owners' wives.

Tubman's rebellion began that same year when she intervened to stop her master from beating an enslaved man who tried to escape. The man threw a metal weight at the slave and hit Tubman in the head instead, breaking her skull. This triggered a lifetime of narcolepsy.

In 1849, she successfully escaped to Philadelphia but returned soon after to rescue her family, eventually assisting in the release of dozens of enslaved people from Maryland. Following the passing of the 1850 Fugitive Slave Act – which stated that escaped slaves should be chased and returned to owners – Tubman, now a part of the Underground Railroad network, would transport escapees north.

During the Civil War in 1861, Tubman worked as a cook and nurse. She led a raid on the Combahee Ferry in South Carolina to free more than 700 enslaved people. Until 1908, she campaigned for women's suffrage. When asked why women should have the vote, she answered, "I have suffered enough to believe it."

Harriet Beecher Stowe

NAME: Harriet Beecher Stowe (1811–1896)
NATIONALITY: American
ACTIVISM: Abolitionist

Harriet Beecher Stowe from Litchfield, Connecticut, first experienced the ideas of social reform when her sister, Catharine, founded one of the first women's schools in the US in 1823, where Stowe studied.

In 1832, she moved to Ohio with her sister and father to become a teacher at another school for female students, also founded by her sister. Here, she began writing, and joined a respected literary group called the Semi-Colon Club, where she met her husband-to-be, Calvin Ellis Stowe. Her new-found network gave her a platform for circulating her writing and in 1843 she published her first book.

At the same time, Stowe began encountering men and women who had escaped from enslavement in nearby Kentucky, a slave state, and found their stories distressing. When the 1850 Fugitive Slave Act was passed – stating that escaped slaves should be captured and returned to owners

– Stowe was even more aware of what would become of the people she was meeting.

Stowe moved to Maine with her husband and six children, but the family faced tremendous sadness when their 18-month-old son died. She would later reveal that the heartbreak helped her to empathize with the unimaginable pain that enslaved mothers felt when their children were forcibly removed from their households.

This inspired Stowe to write her famous novel, *Uncle Tom's Cabin*, which was serialized and then published in 1852. The book sold 300,000 copies in the first year in America and was a great success in the UK, too.

The book stressed the horrific plight of slaves in a way that had not been published before. Stowe's descriptive storytelling helped white readers to understand that slaves, too, felt pain, fear and hope, just as they did. It is speculated that Stowe's work influenced the growing anti-slavery sentiment and the eventual election of President Abraham Lincoln, who passed the Thirteenth Amendment to the Constitution in 1865, abolishing slavery in America.

After the Civil War, the Stowe family purchased an orange grove in Florida and hired former slaves.

THE SUFFRAGE MOVEMENTS (1790–1928)

The global movements to grant women the vote began in the eighteenth century. It took over 130 years for reform to take place.

The timeline below focuses on the movements in the UK, New Zealand and the US.

KEY MOMENTS

1790 – Writer Abigail Adams pioneers the US campaign for women's rights.

1832 – Mary Smith presents the first British women's suffrage petition to Parliament.

1870 – The Fifteenth Amendment to the US Constitution gives black men, not women, the vote.

1889 – British suffragette, Emmeline Pankhurst, leads demonstrations and hunger strikes.

1893 – New Zealand becomes the first country to grant women suffrage.

1894 – The British Local Government Act allows women to vote in council elections.

1908 – 250,000 people attend the Women's Sunday demonstration in London.

1913 – Alice Paul organizes the first major US suffrage march.

1916 – Jeannette Rankin becomes the first woman in the US House of Representatives.

1918 – The British Representation of the People Bill grants married women over 30 the vote.

1919 – Nancy Astor becomes the first female MP in Britain.

1920 – The Nineteenth Amendment, granting American women the vote, is ratified.

1928 – In the UK, the Representation of the People Act is extended to women over 21.

Elizabeth Cady Stanton

NAME: Elizabeth Cady Stanton (1815–1902)
NATIONALITY: American
ACTIVISM: Suffragist and abolitionist

Elizabeth Cady Stanton was introduced to the abolitionist movement at the age of 24, when she met her future husband, journalist Henry Brewster Stanton. The couple married in 1840 and attended the World's Anti-Slavery convention while on their honeymoon in London. To Stanton's disgust, women were excluded from the proceedings, which ignited her fight for equality and led her to become an early leader of the American women's rights movement.

In 1848, Stanton helped to organize the Seneca Falls convention – the first of its kind promoting women's rights. For this, she penned the pivotal "Declaration of Sentiments", in which she demanded social and legal reforms to equalize women's position in society. Stanton went on to campaign for liberal divorce laws, greater sexual freedom and the idea that women should be able to take measures to avoid becoming pregnant.

Stanton met fellow suffragist Susan B. Anthony in 1851 and together they spearheaded the early women's rights movement by travelling around the country to deliver powerful speeches, give political commentary and write articles. Stanton and Anthony's address to the legislature of New York in 1854 secured reforms that allowed women to own property and participate in business transactions, as well as entitling them to secure joint custody of children after divorce.

An alliance was also forming between the suffragists and abolitionists. As the American Civil War began in 1861, Stanton and Anthony heavily petitioned for the Thirteenth Amendment to the US Constitution – the abolition of slavery – which passed in 1865.

By the time she reached her seventies, Stanton had published the first three volumes of *The History of Woman Suffrage*. At the age of 80, she wrote *The Woman's Bible*, urging women to recognize how religion and patriarchy were an obstruction to female empowerment. Stanton passed away in 1902, 18 years before American women were granted the right to vote.

Emmeline Pankhurst

NAME: Emmeline Pankhurst (1858–1928)
NATIONALITY: British
ACTIVISM: Suffragette

Leading British suffragette Emmeline Pankhurst was born into a family of activists. Her mother, Sophia Jane Crane, was a supporter of women's suffrage, while her father, Robert Goulden, campaigned against slavery. Pankhurst's political interest was ignited from a young age.

At just 20 years old, Emmeline met her future husband, Richard Pankhurst, who authored the Married Women's Property Acts of 1870 and 1882. The acts allowed women to keep any money they earned from property before and after marriage. Five children later, and after the death of her husband, Pankhurst founded the Women's Social and Political Union (WSPU) in 1903.

Led by Pankhurst, WSPU members regularly attended demonstrations. They even turned to civil disobedience by heckling politicians, resisting police during rallies and taking part in a series of window-smashing events in London – the latter leading to Pankhurst's arrest.

Detained suffragettes regularly went on hunger strikes in prison, which led to force-feeding. Sketches of these scenes appeared in newspapers and became one of the defining images of the early British suffragette movement, drawing horror and sympathy in equal measure from the public.

In the wake of suffragette Emily Davison being crushed by a royal horse in 1913 (see page 98), Pankhurst spoke openly of the plight women faced, stating, "You have to make more noise than anybody else [...] if you are really going to get your reform realised."

As the First World War began, Pankhurst rallied women to take on the jobs left by men who had gone to fight. By 1918, an estimated two million women gained work – increasing female employment by 13 per cent. Her efforts paid off when the Representation of the People Act was passed, in 1918, granting many women aged 30 and over the right to vote. Ten years later, less than a month after Pankhurst's death, the Act was renewed as the Equal Franchise Act, allowing women over 21 years old to vote.

Kate Sheppard

NAME: Kate Sheppard (1847–1934)
NATIONALITY: New Zealander
ACTIVISM: Suffragist

Liverpool-born Kate Wilson Sheppard emigrated to Christchurch, New Zealand, in her early twenties. There she married and started a family, and began lobbying as one of the country's leading suffragettes. She wrote to newspapers, held public meetings in communities across the North and South Islands, and delivered petitions to parliament asking for reform on several social issues – including banning the sale of alcohol to children.

In 1893, Sheppard collected nearly 32,000 signatures on a petition demanding women's suffrage – leading to the issue being put forward in parliament. As a result, the Electoral Act was passed, making New Zealand the first country to grant women voting rights by law. That year, an incredible 88 per cent of women enrolled to vote in the upcoming election.

Despite her success, Sheppard didn't stop there. In 1896, she became president of the National Council of Women of New Zealand, demanding equal opportunities and pay for women, as well as the right to stand for parliament. She also campaigned heavily for economic independence for married women. Her influence led to her being elected as honorary vice-president of the International Council of Women in 1909.

At the same time, Sheppard continued as editor of *The White Ribbon*, a newspaper created by the Women's Christian Temperance Union (WCTU), published by women for women. Sheppard would regularly discuss issues such as women's economic independence away from men and the need for proportional representation.

Sheppard is still honoured for her society-changing fight, with her face appearing on the New Zealand $10 bill since 1993. In 1993, to mark a centenary of women's suffrage, a memorial was opened in her honour in Christchurch and the annual Kate Sheppard Memorial Trust Award has been introduced for notable women in research.

Emily Davison

NAME: Emily Wilding Davison (1872–1913)
NATIONALITY: British
ACTIVISM: Suffragette

Davison was a young member of the Women's Social and Political Union (WSPU), led by Emmeline Pankhurst, and gave up her role as a teacher to work full-time as an officer and chief steward for the suffragette movement.

She was one of the many women who were arrested for acts of civil disobedience, from burning post boxes to causing public disturbances. She spent short stints in jail – where she took part in hunger strikes and was force-fed on 49 occasions – and even managed to gain entry into the House of Commons and Palace of Westminster to protest.

In June 1913, Davison walked onto the Epsom Derby racetrack during a race, carrying a suffragette flag, and was hit by King George V's horse, Anmer. She died four days later as a result of her injuries. Her funeral was attended by 5,000 suffragettes.

Alice Paul

NAME: Alice Paul (1885–1977)
NATIONALITY: American
ACTIVISM: Suffragist

Alice Paul was a key force behind the campaign that eventually gave American women the vote. As a student in England during the fight for women's suffrage, she endured arrests, imprisonment and hunger strikes alongside her fellow suffragettes.

On her return to America, Paul continued her campaign, becoming a member of the National American Woman Suffrage Association (NAWSA). She organized the nation's first mass rally for women's suffrage in Washington DC on 3 March 1913 to found the Congressional Union for Woman Suffrage, which in 1917 merged with the Woman's Party to form the National Woman's Party. Their dedication pushed for the passing of the Nineteenth Amendment to the US Constitution on 18 August 1920 – granting American women the right to vote.

THE CIVIL RIGHTS MOVEMENT (*c.*1954–1968)

An American movement to end racial discrimination and to allow citizens equal rights under the law, regardless of skin colour.

KEY MOMENTS

1890 – The Jim Crow laws enforce segregation and prevent many African Americans from voting in America's Southern states.

1948 – Racial segregation in the American military is abolished by law.

1954 – The first Civil Rights case reaches the Supreme Court, leading to racial segregation of children in public schools being ruled unconstitutional.

1955 – 14-year-old Emmett Till is lynched in Mississippi, opening many peoples' eyes to the injustices faced by Black people.

1960 – The Supreme Court announces that segregation on public transport is illegal.

1963 – President John F. Kennedy publicly acknowledges that segregation was morally and legally wrong.

1963 – Martin Luther King Jr delivers his "I Have A Dream" speech to 250,000 Americans in Washington DC.

1964 – Muslim minister Malcolm X joins the Civil Rights Movement, challenging the notion of non-violent protest.

1964 – The American Civil Rights Act is passed, outlawing discrimination based on race, colour, religion and sex. Public segregation is also banned.

1965 – Malcolm X is assassinated in New York City.

1965 – The Voting Rights Act makes racial discrimination in voting illegal.

1968 – Martin Luther King Jr is assassinated in Memphis, Tennessee.

1968 – The Fair Housing Act bars discrimination during the rental or sale of housing.

Martin Luther King Jr

NAME: Michael "Martin" Luther King Jr (1929–1968)
NATIONALITY: American
ACTIVISM: Civil rights

Growing up in Georgia, in the midst of segregation, unsurprisingly had a huge impact on Martin Luther King Jr. One of the 15 Southern states that operated under Jim Crow laws, Georgia specified the separation of Black and white people on public buses, in schools, toilets and at shop entrances. King was just six years old when he was told not to play with a white friend because his friend's parents wouldn't allow it.

In 1953, King married singer Coretta Scott and became a pastor in Montgomery, Alabama. Following the arrest of Rosa Parks in 1955 (see page 106) – who failed to give up her seat on the bus to a white man – King organized his first campaign to stand up for African American rights: the Montgomery Bus Boycott.

The boycott was a monumental success. In 1956, after 381 days of protest, the Supreme Court ruled that segregation on public buses was unconstitutional. Unfortunately, King began receiving messages of hate and his family home was firebombed. He was later stabbed in a bookstore.

Inspired by Indian civil rights activist Mahatma Gandhi (see page 110), King continued to protest through non-violence, by attending meetings, giving lectures on African American history, networking with other activists and political leaders, and leading peaceful demonstrations. However, his condoning of civil disobedience – such as sit-ins and marches – during protests against discriminatory hiring practices in Birmingham, Alabama, made him unfavourable to some.

In 1963, King held the March on Washington and, along with other campaigners and religious groups, highlighted the injustices faced by America's Black communities. The march was attended by over 250,000 people and proved to be a breakthrough moment in gaining support for civil rights.

At the end of the march, King delivered his celebrated "I Have a Dream" speech (page 27) from the steps of the Lincoln Memorial in Washington DC. His address called for peace, justice and equality for all Americans. In

1964 – almost 100 years since the abolition of slavery in America – the Civil Rights Act was passed, prohibiting racial segregation and discrimination. In the same year, King's prolific civil rights work won him the Nobel Peace Prize.

Less than a year later, King found himself once again fighting injustice in Selma, Alabama, where violence had erupted between segregationists and peaceful demonstrators. Footage of the situation was shown on television screens across America, horrifying viewers. As a result, supporters came from far and wide to take part in the march from Selma to Montgomery, against discrimination, led by King. In August 1965, the Voting Rights Act was passed, granting all African Americans the vote under the previously established Fifteenth Amendment.

King was shot and killed in April 1968, while standing on the balcony of his motel room in Memphis, Tennessee. His assassination sparked riots across the country, with President Lyndon Johnson declaring a national day of mourning.

Today, King is remembered as a key initiator of the American Civil Rights Movement. His legacy is marked in the US each year on the third Monday in January, a federal holiday known as Martin Luther King Jr Day.

Ruby Bridges

NAME: Ruby Bridges (1954–present)
NATIONALITY: American
ACTIVISM: Civil rights

In November 1960, six-year-old Ruby Bridges became the first African American child to attend elementary school in the Deep South. On arrival at William Frantz Elementary School in New Orleans, Bridges – who was surrounded by US marshals for her own safety – was met by an angry crowd shouting and throwing objects at her.

Despite a court order stating that all schools should be integrated, Bridges spent a year learning alone. Other children had been removed by their parents because of her presence – and only one teacher, Barbara Henry, agreed to teach her. Despite this, Bridges bravely attended school every day with the support of her understandably anxious parents.

Bridges advocates for equality and tolerance to this day.

Rosa Parks

NAME: Rosa Louise Parks (1913–2005)
NATIONALITY: American
ACTIVISM: Civil rights

Fondly thought of as the "mother of the modern-day civil rights movement" in America, Rosa Parks became famous for refusing to surrender her bus seat to a white male passenger. The incident took place in December 1955, in the midst of the Civil Rights Movement. Parks – an established anti-racism activist – had been sitting in the designated "coloured section" of the Montgomery, Alabama, bus when the driver asked her to surrender her seat to the white passenger, as the "white-only" section was full. Parks, who was known for violating Alabama's segregation laws, peacefully exerted her right to remain seated. The action culminated in her arrest.

Her brave act became a defining moment in America's Civil Rights Movement: it empowered African Americans to stand up to the institutionalized racism and racial segregation they faced, and inspired the Montgomery Bus Boycott (see page 102).

Parks, meanwhile, became a symbol of defiance against racial segregation, both in America and the UK, and began working with prominent activists such as Martin Luther King Jr (page 102) and Edgar Nixon. However, she suffered a backlash to her actions, as she received several death threats and was discharged from her job as a seamstress.

In 1965, Parks started a new life in Detroit, Michigan, where she worked as a secretary for US Representative John Conyers Jr. In 1987, she co-founded the Rosa and Raymond Parks Institute for Self-Development in memory of her husband, who had passed away ten years earlier. The institute was set up to educate young people on the Black history of America and inspire them to stand up for positive change.

Upon retiring in 1988, Parks wrote her autobiography: *Rosa Parks: My Story* (1992), along with three more books, including a children's hardback on her activism. She received the Congressional Gold Medal in 1999 and asked Pope John Paul II for racial healing at their meeting in 2000. She passed away peacefully in 2005.

ACTIVISTS WHO CHANGED THE COURSE OF HISTORY

A selection of important turning points in activist history.

REFORMS TO REMEMBER

1935 – The US Social Security Act is established for the elderly, unemployed and disadvantaged.

1938 – Activist John Patten holds a national day of mourning to mark the takeover of aboriginal land in Australia.

1938 – The American Fair Labor Standards Act bans child labour, and asserts maximum working hours and a minimum wage.

1947 – Mahatma Gandhi leads India into independence from British rule.

1962 – Indigenous people are granted the vote in Australia's federal elections.

1965 – The UK Race Relations Act is announced; it is the first UK policy to address racial discrimination.

1968 – An amendment to the aforementioned Race Relations Act prevents workplace, housing and public service discrimination based on race.

1993 – Ruth Bader Ginsburg becomes the second woman elected to the US Supreme Court.

1994 – Nelson Mandela is appointed president of South Africa, formally ending apartheid.

2009 – The Lilly Ledbetter Fair Pay Act, prompted by Ruth Bader Ginsburg, ensures equal pay for all.

2015 – Same-sex marriage is made legal throughout the United States.

Mahatma Gandhi

NAME: Mohandas Karamchand "Mahatma" Gandhi
  (1869–1948)
NATIONALITY: Indian
ACTIVISM: Anti-colonialist

Having qualified as a barrister, Gandhi moved from India to South Africa in 1893. It was here, at 25 years old, that he made the change to political activist, after witnessing the racial discrimination experienced by South Africa's Indian community. For 20 years, he battled against a political system that did not allow South African Indians voting rights, drawing international awareness to their plight.

In 1915, Gandhi returned to India to lead the movement for civil rights, religious freedom and "Swaraj" (independence) from the British Raj government. As Congress leader, he put forward demands for liberation, which were rejected by the British. In response, Gandhi encouraged acts of civil disobedience, particularly demonstrations and boycotts of British products. This prompted the Rowlatt Act, authorizing the arrest of anyone acting against the Crown.

In a show of conscious activism, Gandhi lived a modest life to match working-class society. He wore a dhoti – a traditional hand-woven loincloth – so that he could identify with low-income communities. He also encouraged small movements against poverty, land tax and prejudice, and argued for equality for women.

When tensions between British rulers and the Indian people spiralled, Gandhi was arrested for entering Delhi to protest. While in prison, Gandhi began regular fasts – a signature tactic that gained international attention. His final fast, aged 78, took place as British rule ended. The Raj released 100,000 political prisoners after the Second World War and independence was granted in August 1947. Gandhi was assassinated five months later.

Though he did a lot of good in the world, some have questioned his status as a moral authority, given controversial statements he made about sex and race.

Frances Perkins

NAME: Frances Perkins (1880–1965)
NATIONALITY: American
ACTIVISM: Workers' rights

Frances Perkins's interest in social reform began after witnessing the unfavourable working conditions faced by factory staff during a tour. After teaching chemistry in Massachusetts, she studied economics at the University of Pennsylvania, before moving to New York to gain a second degree. Her first major role came in 1910, when – as head of the New York office of the National Consumers League – she petitioned for better working hours and conditions.

In 1911, disaster struck in the form of the devastating Triangle Shirtwaist Factory fire. Many workers tried to flee but, sadly, 146 people – mostly young women – died because of the lack of fire escapes. The tragic event rattled Perkins to her core and convinced her to leave the National Consumers League to become the executive secretary for the Committee on Safety for New York. Here, she successfully campaigned for the "fifty-four-hour bill" – a law capping the number of hours women and children could work per week.

After her marriage and the birth of her daughter, Perkins became one of the first female commissioners of New York in 1919, and she was promoted to being the inaugural New York state industrial commissioner in 1929. In this role, Perkins reduced the working week for women to 48 hours and instated unemployment insurance laws. She also campaigned to end child labour.

When Franklin Roosevelt was elected as president of the United States in 1933, he asked Perkins to join his cabinet as Secretary of Labor. She agreed, providing he would support her reforms. With Roosevelt's backing, Perkins helped to create the Civilian Conservation Corps and She-She-She Camps, which provided relief for unemployed men and women. She also helped to draft the Social Security Act of 1935 and write the New Deal legislation of federal programmes to assist America's recovery from the Great Depression. In 1938, the Fair Labor Standards Act was passed, establishing maximum working hours and a minimum wage, and banning child labour.

John Patten

NAME: John Thomas Patten (1905–1957)
NATIONALITY: Australian
ACTIVISM: Human rights

When John Patten co-founded the Aborigines Progressive Association (APA) in 1937, he hoped to establish human rights for his fellow indigenous Australians. The date of 26 January 1788 marked the day when British colonizers arrived, which led to the violent takeover of the aboriginal peoples' land. As his first mission as APA President, Patten organized the Day of Mourning protest in January 1938 to mark the 150th anniversary since this event. Although the day is celebrated as "Australia Day" by most Australians of European descent, it remains an annual day of mourning among aboriginal communities.

The first win of Patten's campaign came when indigenous people were accepted into the armed forces. He regularly attended events, speaking extensively on civil rights – or the lack thereof – alongside fellow activist Pearl Gibbs. In 1939, he addressed the Cummeragunja community in New South Wales, informing them of the impending government plan to forcibly remove aboriginal children from their families and give them to white Australians. Residents fled the area. Patten was arrested for his actions.

Patten's work paved the way for current-day activists who continue to challenge the federal government to change "Australia Day" celebrations to a date that isn't as traumatic for indigenous Australians.

IF THERE IS NO STRUGGLE, THERE IS NO PROGRESS.

FREDERICK DOUGLASS,
SOCIAL REFORMER, ABOLITIONIST
AND WRITER

Paul Stephenson OBE

NAME: Paul Stephenson OBE (1937–present)
NATIONALITY: British
ACTIVISM: Anti-racism

From 1955 to 1964, the employment of Black and Asian workers was unofficially prohibited by Bristol's nationalized bus company. In 1963, social worker Paul Stephenson organized a 60-day bus boycott against the company, attracting media attention and encouraging thousands of people to support the grassroots movement. Thanks to significant public pressure, it transpired that the Transport and General Workers' Union had covertly brought in the prohibition policy.

Six months later, as Martin Luther King Jr delivered his "I Have a Dream" speech in Washington, the Bristol Omnibus Company lifted the colour bar. A month later, Raghbir Singh, a Sikh Bristolian, became the first non-white bus conductor in the city. Stephenson's courage paved the way for the Race Relations Act of 1965, prohibiting discrimination based on colour, race and ethnic origin.

Nelson Mandela

NAME: Nelson Rolihlahla Mandela (1918–2013)
NATIONALITY: South African
ACTIVISM: Civil rights

From an early age, Nelson Mandela strove to improve the circumstances of the Black community. Apartheid sanctioned racial segregation between South Africa's majority Black and minority white communities, and supported discrimination against non-white people. So, in 1944, Mandela joined the African National Congress (ANC) party in order to stand against this policy.

Following the implementation of the 1950 Population Registration Act – which categorized all South Africans as either Bantu (Black), coloured (mixed race) or white (of European descent) – further policies were introduced, which created sectioned living and working regions for each group, with only white South Africans being allowed to venture out of their boundary.

Mandela opened South Africa's first Black law firm in 1952 and led the ANC's campaign for the Defiance of Unjust Laws, organizing boycotts, strikes and passive protests to seek reform on the discriminatory policies aimed at Black communities.

In 1960, police killed 69 Black protestors during a peaceful demonstration, which triggered riots across the country. The ANC was banned by the government as a result, forcing Mandela and his activists to operate underground. Shortly after, when an ANC refuge in Johannesburg was raided, evidence was found connecting Mandela to the now-guerrilla insurgency. He was jailed for life, and his parting address was the now-famous speech "I Am Prepared to Die". Many governments – including the United States – imposed economic sanctions to pressure the South African government into ending apartheid, although, for many years, little changed.

Mandela was released from prison in 1990 and became a presidential nominee for South Africa's first-ever election in which persons of all races could vote. He became the country's first Black president, officially ending apartheid in 1994. Mandela championed social justice until his death, aged 95, in 2013.

Ruth Bader Ginsburg

NAME: Ruth Bader Ginsburg (1933–2020)
NATIONALITY: American
ACTIVISM: Equal rights

Ruth Bader Ginsburg knew she wanted to work in law from a young age. She enrolled at Harvard Law School – where she was one of only nine women in a class of 500 men. After graduating from Cornell University, she married Martin "Marty" Ginsburg and completed her education at Columbia Law School.

Ginsburg began her career at the Oklahoma Social Security Administration, where she soon experienced sexism when she was demoted for becoming pregnant. "Not a law firm in the entire city of New York would employ me," she later explained. "I struck out on three grounds: I was Jewish, a woman and a mother."

Yet Ginsburg persevered, eventually going on to become co-founder of the *Women's Rights Law*

Reporter in 1970 – the first American law journal to specifically address female entitlements. This led to the establishment of the Women's Rights Project at the American Civil Liberties Union (ACLU) in 1972. By 1974, the project had represented more than 300 gender discrimination cases.

Ginsburg went on to become one of the ACLU's most influential assets and provided valuable counsel during gender discrimination cases. Her method was to carefully explain the issue to the all-male judges, pointing out that they, too, would benefit from equality. She addressed as many discriminatory laws and policies as she could manage, slowly chipping away at America's gender-biased legal system.

It was this incredible résumé that led to Ginsburg being nominated to the US Court of Appeals for District of Columbia by President Jimmy Carter, and then to the Supreme Court in 1993 by President Bill Clinton. She became the second woman confirmed to the bench, after Sandra Day O'Connor. As justice, she fought hard to end gender discrimination, challenging state-run Virginia Military Institute's male-only policy and supporting abortion rights. Under President Barack Obama, Ginsburg updated the Lilly Ledbetter Fair Pay Act, ensuring that gender bias at work was inexcusable by law. She also voted to legalize same-sex marriage in all 50 states in 2015.

Ginsburg's formidable work as a Supreme Court justice slowly transformed her into an international icon. She held her position for 27 years, until her death in September 2020.

FIGHT FOR THE THINGS THAT YOU CARE ABOUT, BUT DO IT IN A WAY THAT WILL LEAD OTHERS TO JOIN YOU.

RUTH BADER GINSBURG,
SUPREME COURT JUSTICE OF THE
UNITED STATES OF AMERICA

A NEW GENERATION OF EVERYDAY HEROES

Across the world, people are on an unwavering quest for change. Their work is having an extraordinary impact on us today.

MODERN-DAY ACTIVISM IN ACTION

1972 – US journalist Gloria Steinem launches the first feminist-themed magazine, *Ms.*

1999 – Baroness Doreen Lawrence begins her battle for justice for the victims of racial crime, after the murder of her son Stephen.

2013 – The Black Lives Matter movement is established by Alicia Garza, Patrisse Cullors and Opal Tometi.

2013 – The Malala Fund, founded by Malala Yousafzai, begins its campaign for free education for girls in eight underprivileged countries.

2017 – Journalist Behrouz Boochani's smartphone documentary, *Chauka, Please Tell Us the Time*, exposes the cruelty of Australian offshore immigration detention centres.

2017 – Activist Elle Hearns addresses thousands of protestors at the Washington DC Women's March, promoting Black transgender rights.

2017 – The phrase and movement #MeToo was originally founded in 2006 by Tarana Burke (see page 136). In 2017 it went viral thanks to a tweet by Alyssa Milano, launching a worldwide campaign to highlight the prevalence of sexual harassment and abuse.

2018 – 15-year-old Greta Thunberg protests for climate action outside the Swedish parliament.

2020 – Black Lives Matter protests take place globally to oppose police brutality.

2020 – Footballer Marcus Rashford successfully campaigns for the UK government to provide free school meals to children over school holidays during the coronavirus pandemic.

Gloria Steinem

NAME: Gloria Steinem (1934–present)
NATIONALITY: American
ACTIVISM: Women's rights

In 1969, Steinem published an article in *New York Magazine* entitled "After Black Power, Women's Liberation"; unexpectedly, the piece propelled her into the public eye, starting her on her journey as an advocate for women's rights.

In 1971, her speech at the National Women's Political Caucus (NWPC) furthered the notion of the American feminist movement, stating how sex and race were conveniently used to organize levels of superiority. In 1972, Steinem co-founded the first American feminist-themed magazine, entitled Ms., in which she wrote broadly about women's rights and issues. The first issue of the magazine sold out its 300,000 copies within eight days.

Even today, in her eighties, Steinem shows no sign of wishing to retire from campaigning.

Elle Hearns

NAME: Elle Hearns (1986–present)
NATIONALITY: American
ACTIVISM: Transgender rights

Growing up as a young Black boy was an uncomfortable and turbulent time for Elle Hearns. It took many years for her to realize she was transgender, a transition that relieved her insecurity. She helped to launch the Black Lives Matter network, using her platform as organizing director to highlight the struggle of Black transgender people. As executive director of the Marsha P. Johnson Institute – set up to end violence against all transgender people – Hearns led a National Day of Action in 2015, in response to the murders of several Black transgender women.

Her inspirational address at the 2017 Women's March in Washington DC – describing the sisterhood between transgender and cisgender Black women – brought an unspoken camaraderie to the crowd. As a speaker, writer and strategist, Hearns continues her quest to empower, defend and protect the lives of all transgender people.

Doreen Lawrence OBE

NAME: Doreen Lawrence OBE (1949–present)
NATIONALITY: British
ACTIVISM: Anti-racism

Sometimes it takes a heart-breaking event to transform someone into an activist. For Doreen Lawrence, it was the tragic murder of her son (Stephen) in a racist attack in 1993. The ensuing police investigation failed to charge anyone for the murder, despite five prime suspects from a known racist gang being named. At the time, Lawrence and her husband labelled the investigation prejudiced and incompetent. The British news media launched a campaign for justice.

A 1999 public inquiry into the case, chaired by Sir William MacPherson, concluded that the Metropolitan Police was "institutionally racist". It also recommended that the rule of double jeopardy – where an accused person, if acquitted, cannot be tried for the same crime twice – be retracted in murder cases. British law was changed as a result.

After the verdict, Lawrence campaigned for reform in the police service, calling for structural changes so that the victims of racist crimes could have renewed faith in the Metropolitan Police. This inspiring work in the wake of heartache earned Lawrence an OBE in 2003, and she was invited to become a panellist at police service and British Home Office discussions, to ensure that racism was addressed openly.

In 2012, two of the five suspects were trialled and found guilty of Stephen Lawrence's murder. They were sentenced to life in prison with minimum terms. In 2014, an independent review into the case and undercover policing unveiled corruption, with plans to smear the grieving mother's initial battle for justice.

Her endless campaigning for reform gained Lawrence the title of Baroness, as well as a Lifetime Achievement Award at the Pride of Britain Awards.

The Stephen Lawrence Charitable Trust, set up by Lawrence, offers support to young people from disadvantaged backgrounds to reach further education and employment. Baroness Lawrence became the race relations advisor of the British Labour Party in 2020.

Behrouz Boochani

NAME: Behrouz Boochani (1983–present)
NATIONALITY: Kurdish-Iranian
ACTIVISM: Human rights

At 30 years of age, Behrouz Boochani found himself on a boat with 60 other refugees, crossing the strait from Indonesia to Australia. He left his home in Iran after the office of the magazine he co-founded was raided by the Islamic Revolutionary Guard, to stop Boochani and his team from speaking out about political and social injustice. After three months in hiding, he fled to Indonesia.

The boat was intercepted by the Royal Australian Navy, and Boochani and his fellow asylum seekers were taken to an island for holding. He would later find out that Manus Island was where all single male refugees were taken. He had become a part of Australia's Pacific Solution policy, which sees maritime asylum seekers put into offshore detention while their immigration status is determined.

In detention, Boochani witnessed the ill treatment of refugees and filmed evidence of the human rights abuses many of them faced. Using a concealed mobile phone, he sent it to advocacy groups and news organizations, exposing the plight of asylum seekers coming to Australia.

Boochani became a spokesperson for detainees, writing articles via text messages to describe experiences such as solitary confinement in shipping containers, hunger strikes and peaceful protests. Meanwhile, human rights groups launched an international campaign to persuade the Australian government to adopt fairer policies in processing asylum seekers. Journalist Ben Doherty, who collected an Amnesty International Award on Boochani's behalf in 2017, stated how Boochani "rightly sees himself as a working journalist on Manus Island, whose job it is to bear witness to the injustices and the violence and the privation of offshore detention".

In 2017 Boochani's documentary, *Chauka, Please Tell Us the Time,* was released, containing six months' worth of smartphone footage of life in detention. In November 2019, Boochani was granted refugee status by the New Zealand government. He continues to campaign for the 79.5 million displaced people fighting for safety.

Alicia Garza

NAME: Alicia Garza (1981–present)
NATIONALITY: American
ACTIVISM: Anti-racism

California-born Alicia Garza has been speaking about birth control, sex education and higher wages for workers since her student days. In 2012, while brainstorming with friends Opal Tometi and Patrisse Cullors, Garza commented on the murderer of unarmed black teenager, Trayvon Martin, being acquitted, stating: "I continue to be surprised at how little Black lives matter." The observation launched the international Black Lives Matter movement, which seeks reform against institutionalized racism and police brutality against Black people.

Garza also established the US organization Black Futures Lab, which educates and empowers Black communities to register and vote in elections. She currently oversees Special Projects at the US National Domestic Workers Alliance.

Malala Yousafzai

NAME: Malala Yousafzai (1997–present)
NATIONALITY: Pakistani
ACTIVISM: Female education

Malala Yousafzai was 12 years old when she wrote her first article describing life under Taliban rule for BBC Urdu. It was read around the world, and a *New York Times* documentary was made about her experiences. The Taliban responded by shooting her in the head when she was on a bus. After life-saving treatment in Pakistan, she was taken to the UK for refuge and recovery.

Yousafzai now uses her platform to campaign for free female education. The Malala Fund aims to provide 12 years of learning for every girl in Afghanistan, Brazil, Ethiopia, India, Lebanon, Nigeria, Pakistan and Turkey. In 2014, the fund helped to build an all-girls high school in Kenya and created makeshift classrooms in Sierra Leone for girls who were unable to attend school during the Ebola virus outbreak. That same year Malala was named co-recipient of the Nobel Peace Prize.

Greta Thunberg

NAME: Greta Thunberg (2003–present)
NATIONALITY: Swedish
ACTIVISM: Environmentalist

At the age of just 15, Greta Thunberg did something amazing: she began campaigning for more action on climate change outside the Swedish parliament... on a school day. She took with her a simple sign which read *Skolstrejk för klimatet* ("School strike for climate"). Her efforts gained local coverage and encouraged other students to organize similar protests.

She was invited to the 2018 United Nations (UN) Climate Change Conference alongside experienced activists such as Sir David Attenborough. In her address, Thunberg declared: "What I hope we achieve at this conference is that we realize that we are facing an existential threat. This is the biggest crisis humanity has ever faced."

Her empowering address encouraged students all over the world to strike, and peaceful demonstrations took place in cities globally throughout 2019. It's estimated that over a million students joined the movement in 125 countries. The message to politicians was simple: use your power to reduce climate change and save the planet for future generations.

To make her point further, and to appease critics, Thunberg sailed across the Atlantic Ocean, rather than flying, to attend the 2019 UN Climate Action summit in New York. Her powerful speech, "How Dare You" (see page 27), was shared globally and received vast media coverage.

During her campaigning, rumours surfaced about her upbringing and mental health. Her parents addressed this by admitting that, although they didn't initially support their daughter's requests to lower the family's carbon footprint, they now understand the significance of her actions.

Thunberg is the youngest winner of *Time* magazine's Person of the Year, appeared on the *Forbes* list of The World's 100 Most Powerful Women and was nominated for the Nobel Peace Prize. In 2019, she addressed public speculation of her Asperger diagnosis by writing on Instagram: "I have Asperger's syndrome and that means I'm sometimes a bit different from the norm. And – given the right circumstances – being different is a superpower."

Tarana Burke

NAME: Tarana Burke (1973–present)
NATIONALITY: American
ACTIVISM: Women's and civil rights

At just 16 years old, Tarana worked with young victims of sexual violence from deprived and marginalized New York communities, allowing the girls to share their suffering and to begin healing.

In 2006, Burke created the Just Be Inc. programme after meeting a young girl who had been sexually abused. The programme promotes wellness in young Black girls between the ages of 12 and 18, and discusses the prevalence of sexual abuse. Later, Burke admitted she wished she had responded to the girl, to show her understanding, by saying: "Me too."

The phrase "me too" inspired victims of sexual abuse and assault to realize they were not alone in their suffering and, slowly, a movement was established. In 2017, the hashtag #MeToo went viral – and today it continues to encourage and empower women all over the world to open up about their experiences.

Marcus Rashford

NAME: Marcus Rashford (1997–present)
NATIONALITY: British
ACTIVISM: Anti-poverty

With schools closed in the midst of the first coronavirus pandemic lockdown, news emerged that 2.4 million British children were living in food-insecure households, and that many were missing regular food because they were no longer receiving their free school meals during the school holidays.

Upon hearing this, Manchester United football player Marcus Rashford, 22, penned an open letter to Parliament, asking for the extension of the meal policy to all children in need. After initially declining the request, the government agreed to his proposal, ensuring that countless children didn't starve over the summer. In a matter of weeks, Rashford was joined by top brands and supermarkets in calling for an independent review of UK food policy.

Rashford continues to campaign and says his mission is to end child poverty in Britain.

Conclusion

We owe so much to the brave activists who have campaigned to give us, and generations to come, a fair and just future. This guide has introduced you to some of the greats – but it has only scratched the surface. History is full of these incredible people; many of them went above and beyond their duty as ordinary citizens, leaving legacies in the form of democracy and social justice. Others have quietly and confidently made their mark through education and awareness, contributing toward the more informed and open-minded society we live in today.

In this book, we have seen how activism is, for the most part, not an act of rebellion. Instead, it's the act of bringing people together, often to create a safer and more inclusive culture for everyone. While some acts of civil disobedience have given activism a controversial reputation, we have seen that most activists only seek to build a kind and compassionate community – one where we consider each other as equal, and where we all do our part to care for and protect our world.

Hopefully by reading the motivational accounts of other activists, you will find yourself inspired to advocate for the causes that you care about. Perhaps there is an issue that has already touched your life – or maybe, having read about the injustice faced by others, you are now ready to step up as an ally.

If a fire has been ignited, you now have a catalogue of creative actions that can be used to support the issues that matter in a way that feels most true to you. And, if you're willing, you can learn more about the social, political, economic and environmental concerns we face as human beings by using the list of wonderful and varied resources at the end of this book. Remember: the only thing you need to be an activist is a genuine desire for change.

Finally, let's salute the activists who are out there today, educating us about important causes and continuing the campaign for reform – these are the real-life heroes who will, in time, help us to achieve the better world we all hope for. Maybe one day soon, you will be one, too.

Resources

If this book has been inspiring and you would like to explore the topic of activism even further, the following resources are a great place to start.

ACTIVISM

Christopher Kush, *The One-Hour Activist* (2007)

Gina Martin, *Be the Change* (2019)

Hillary Rettig, *Lifelong Activist: How to Change the World Without Losing Your Way* (2005)

Kajal Odedra, *Do Something: Activism for Everyone* (2019)

Kate and Ella Robertson, *How to Make a Difference: The Definitive Guide from the World's Most Effective Activists* (2019)

Naomi Klein, *No Is Not Enough* (2018)

Ruby Bridges, *This Is Your Time* (2020)

BOOKS ON ACTIVISTS AND MOVEMENTS

Alicia Garza, *The Purpose of Power: How We Come Together When We Fall Apart* (2020)

Elaine Weiss, *The Woman's Hour* (2018)

Lisa Gail Collins (editor) and Margo Natalie Crawford (editor), *New Thoughts on the Black Arts Movement* (2006)

Mark Steeds, *Cry Freedom, Cry Seven Stars: Thomas Clarkson in Bristol, 1787* (2008)

Mary Wollstonecraft, *A Vindication of the Rights of Woman* (1792, revised edition 2004)

Mike Berners-Lee, *There Is No Planet B* (2019)

Rosa Parks and Jim Haskins, *Rosa Parks: My Story* (1992)

Ruth Bader Ginsburg, *My Own Words* (2016)

FILMS AND TELEVISION

A Life on Our Planet, narrated by David Attenborough (2020)

An Inconvenient Truth, directed by Davis Guggenheim (2006)

Bowling for Columbine, written and directed by Michael Moore (2002)

Cries from Syria, directed by Evgeny Afineevsky (2017)

Girl Rising, directed by Richard E. Robbins (2013)

Selma, directed by Ava DuVernay (2014)

To Kill a Mockingbird, directed by Robert Mulligan (1962)

Utopia, directed by John Pilger and Alan Lowery (2013)

We Are Many, directed by Amir Amirani (2014)

When They See Us, directed by Ava DuVernay (2019)